The Pizza Party

Learning Basic Problem-Solving Skills

Grace Pezzimenti

Rosen Classroom Books & Materials
New York

I am having a birthday party!

10 pieces

My mom gets a pizza for the party. The pizza has 10 pieces.

10 pieces − 4 pieces = 6 pieces

Four people come to the party. If each of them eats 1 piece of pizza, how many pieces are left?

6 pieces − 2 pieces = 4 pieces

Two more people come to the party. If they both eat 1 piece of pizza, how many pieces are left?

4 pieces − 3 pieces = 1 piece

Three more people come to the party. If each of them eats 1 piece of pizza, how many pieces are left?

1 piece − 1 piece = 0 pieces

If I eat 1 piece of pizza, how many pieces are left?

1 + 1 + 1 + 1 + 1 = 5 pieces

Five more people come to the party. If each person wants 1 piece of pizza, how many pieces will we need?

We have to get another pizza. Now we have 10 more pieces of pizza.

10 pieces − 5 pieces = ?

Five people each eat 1 piece of pizza.
How many pieces are left?

10 pieces − 5 pieces = 5 pieces

There are 5 pieces of pizza left!

Words to Know

party

pizza